1948 U.K. YEARBOOK

ISBN: 9781790333103

© Liberty Eagle Publishing Ltd. 2017
All Rights Reserved

	Page
People In High Office	4
Events	8
Births - UK Personalities	17
Popular Music	23
Top 5 Films	29
Sporting Winners	45
Cost Of Living	52

FIRST EDITION

People In High Office

King George VI
Reign: 11th December 1936 - 6th February 1952
Predecessor: Edward VIII / Successor: Elizabeth II

Prime Minister

Clement Attlee
Labour Party
26th July 1945 - 26th October 1951

Australia

Canada

United States

Prime Minister
Ben Chifley
Labor Party
13th July 1945
- 19th December 1949

Prime Minister
Mackenzie King
Liberal Party
23rd October 1935
- 15th November 1948

President
Harry S. Truman
Democratic Party
12th April 1945
- 20th January 1953

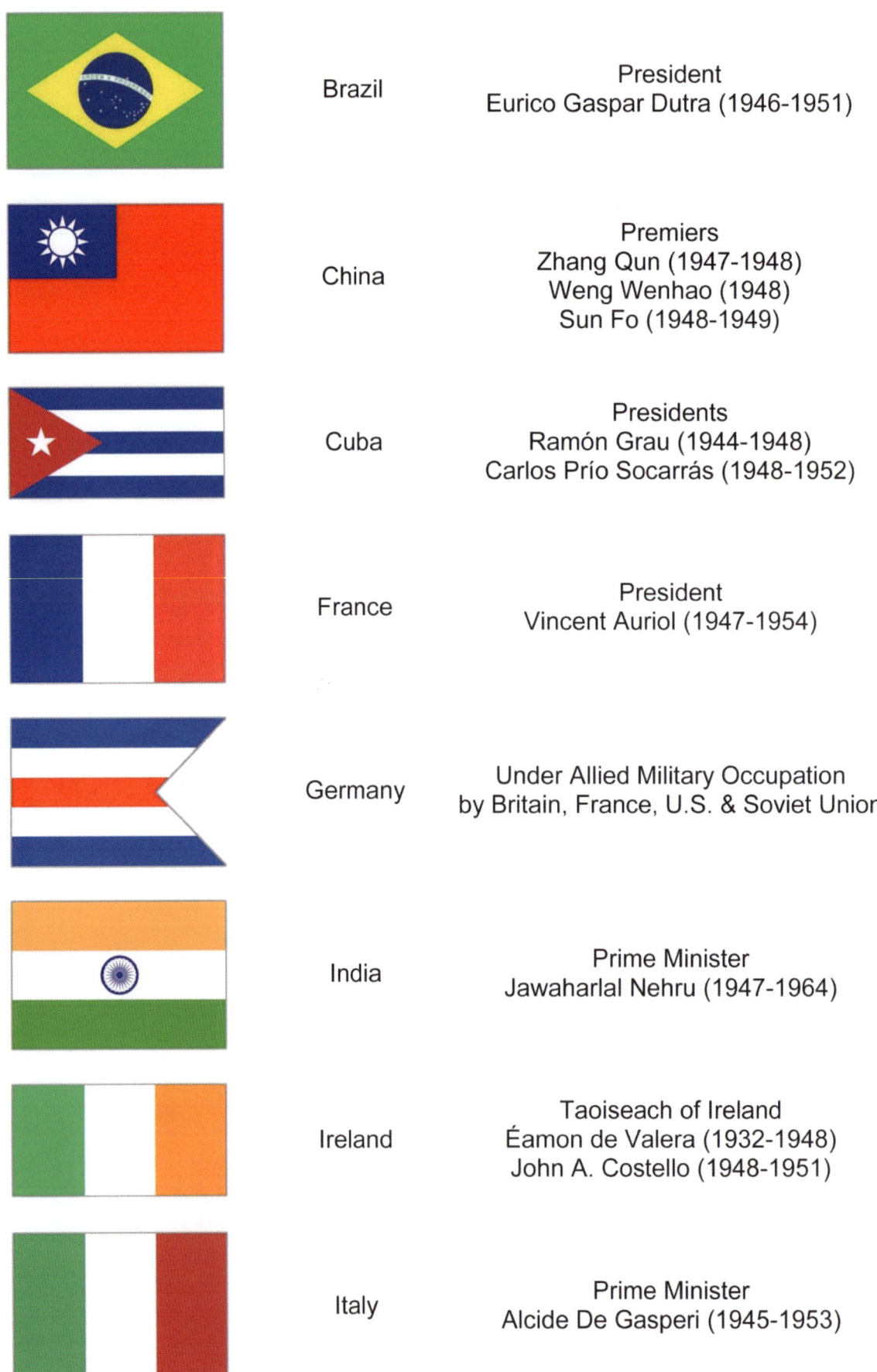

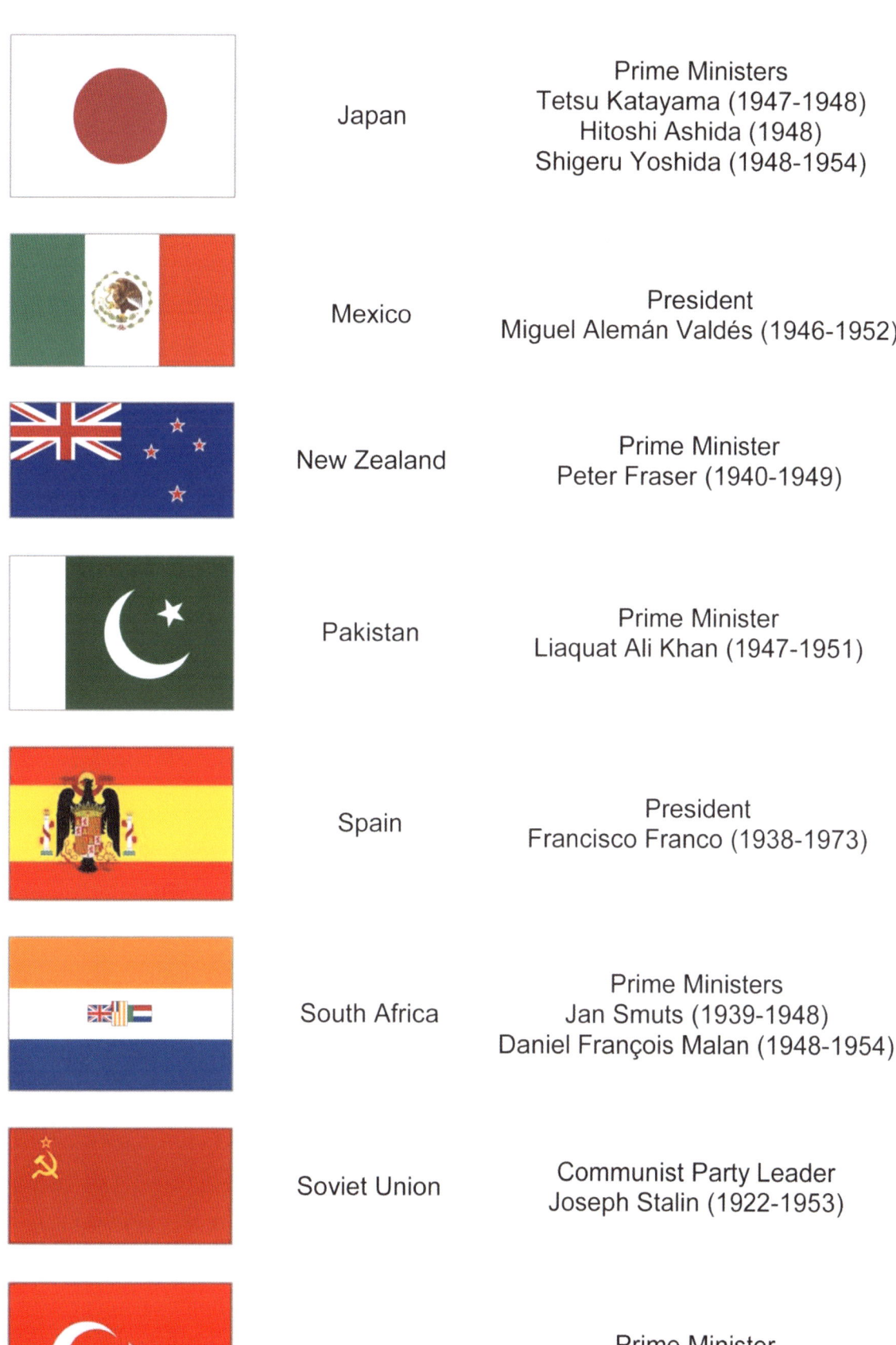

Country	Leader(s)
Japan	Prime Ministers Tetsu Katayama (1947-1948) Hitoshi Ashida (1948) Shigeru Yoshida (1948-1954)
Mexico	President Miguel Alemán Valdés (1946-1952)
New Zealand	Prime Minister Peter Fraser (1940-1949)
Pakistan	Prime Minister Liaquat Ali Khan (1947-1951)
Spain	President Francisco Franco (1938-1973)
South Africa	Prime Ministers Jan Smuts (1939-1948) Daniel François Malan (1948-1954)
Soviet Union	Communist Party Leader Joseph Stalin (1922-1953)
Turkey	Prime Minister Hasan Saka (1947-1949)

Events from 1948

January

1st	The government nationalises the railway industry creating British Railways.
4th	Burma gains its independence from the United Kingdom.
5th	The first episode of the radio serial drama Mrs Dale's Diary is broadcast on the BBC Light Programme (the Light Programme was rebranded as Radio 2 in 1967).
12th	The London Co-operative Society opens Britain's first supermarket in Manor Park, London. Later in January Marks & Spencer also introduce self-service in the food department of their London Wood Green store.
17th	An all-time record attendance is achieved for an English Football League game as 83,260 people watch Manchester United draw with Arsenal at Maine Road.
30th - 8th Feb	Great Britain and Northern Ireland compete in the Winter Olympics at St. Moritz, Switzerland winning 2 bronze medals.

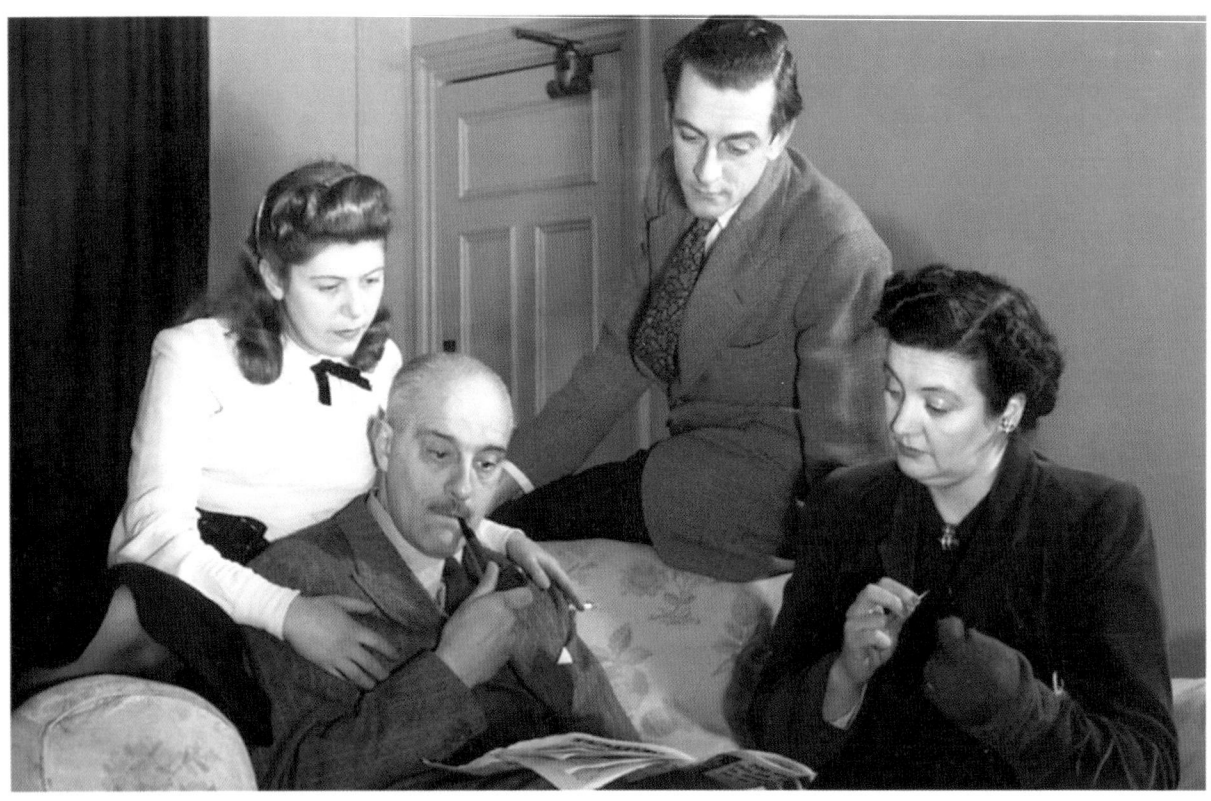

On the 5th January BBC Radio's Light Programme broadcast the first episode of Mrs Dale's Diary - a radio drama serial centred around the daily diary of a doctor's wife called Mary, her husband Jim, (who provided the show with its unlikely catchphrase, 'I'm rather worried about Jim') and their children, Bob and Gwen. For the following twenty one years and 5,531 episodes up to 6 million listeners tuned in every day between 11.00am and 11.15am to hear the everyday affairs of this much loved family. The lead character, Mrs Dale, was played by Ellis Powell until she was sacked in controversial circumstances in 1963 and replaced by Jessie Matthews.

FEBRUARY

4th — Ceylon (now Sri Lanka) becomes independent within the British Commonwealth. George VI becomes King of Ceylon.

6th — John Sankey, 1st Viscount Sankey (born 26th October 1866) dies. Sankey was a lawyer, judge, Labour politician and the Lord Chancellor of Great Britain. He was famous for many of his judgments in the House of Lords and gave his name to the 1940 Sankey Declaration of the Rights of Man, which was widely publicised at the time. This has since been largely forgotten having been overtaken by the Universal Declaration of Human Rights.

MARCH

The Trades Union Congress and Government agree a formal policy of voluntary wage restraint.

The Administrative Staff College (established in 1945) runs its first courses at Greenlands, Henley-on-Thames and is the UK's first business school. Now renamed the Henley Business School it is ranked among the world's top 50 by the Financial Times and The Economist.

The 'New Look' in women's fashion becomes available in British stores. Launched by Christian Dior in 1947, the New Look became extremely popular as a refreshing antidote to the austerity of wartime. It was embraced by a number of prominent clients from Hollywood and the European aristocracy including the likes of Princess Margaret in the UK.

17th — Britain signs the Treaty of Brussels with Belgium, France, Luxembourg and the Netherlands.

23rd — The radio comedy 'Take It From Here', written by Frank Muir and Denis Norden, is first broadcast by the BBC. Reinventing British post-war radio comedy it would run for 13 series (328 episodes) until the 3rd March 1960.

23rd — Group Captain John Cunningham sets a new world altitude record.

Group Captain John Cunningham with his modified Vampire F.1 fighter aircraft.

During a 45-minute flight over Hatfield, Hertfordshire the de Havilland Aircraft Company chief test pilot, Group Captain John 'Cat's Eyes' Cunningham, DSO, flew a modified DH.100 Vampire F.1 fighter to a Fédération Aéronautique Internationale (FAI) World Record for Altitude of 18,119 meters (59,445.5 feet) - beating the record set ten years earlier by Colonel Mario Pezzi in his Caproni Ca.161 biplane. In 1949 Cunningham notably went on to fly the world's first ever jet airliner, the de Havilland Comet.

APRIL

- 1st — The nationalisation of the electricity supply industry comes into effect under the terms of the Electricity Act 1947.
- 1st — Fire services in the UK return to control of local authorities from the National Fire Service.
- 15th — Rowntree's introduce Polo mint sweets.
- 16th — The Australian cricket team arrive in England and during the subsequent tour do not lose a single match. Captained by Don Bradman this feat earned them the nickname of The Invincibles and they are regarded as one of the greatest cricket teams of all time.
- 24th — Manchester United defeat Blackpool 4-2 in the FA Cup final at Wembley Stadium to claim their first major trophy for 37 years.
- 30th — The first Land Rover was officially launched at the Amsterdam Motor Show. On the 8th May 2007 the 4,000,000th Land Rover rolled off the production line and was donated to The Born Free Foundation. The Land Rover is regarded as a British icon and was granted a Royal Warrant by George VI in 1951.

Early 1948 advertisements for Rowntree's new Polo mint.

Rowntree's developed the Polo mint in 1939 but rationing saw its introduction delayed until 1948. First manufactured by employee John Bargewell at their Factory in York, Polo's were very similar to Life Savers which had been introduced in the U.S. in 1912 and Britain in 1916. Because no action had been taken to protect the rights of Life Savers Rowntree's was free to introduce its own version (preventing legal action by clearly stating 'Made by Rowntree's' on the packaging). The Polo followed a wave of innovations during the 1930's at Rowntree's that included Aero, Smarties and the Kit Kat.

MAY

4th	Sir Laurence Olivier's film of Shakespeare's Hamlet is released. It will be the first British film (and the first non-Hollywood production) to win the Academy Award for Best Picture. Olivier himself also wins an Oscar for Best Actor for his role in the film.
13th	The government introduces the National Assistance Act and formally abolishes the Poor Law system that had existed since the reign of Elizabeth I.
14th	The murder of June Anne Devaney, a three-year-old girl from Blackburn, leads to the fingerprinting of 46,253 males aged over 16 from the Blackburn area. It is the first time that a mass fingerprinting operation had been undertaken and on the 12th August 1948 a match was made with ex-serviceman Peter Griffiths. Griffiths was found guilty and hanged at Liverpool Prison on the 19th November 1948. Afterwards Blackburn police, as promised, destroyed all the sets of fingerprints.
14th	At midnight the British Mandate of Palestine is officially terminated and the state of Israel comes into being.

JUNE

	Professor Lillian Penson becomes the first woman elected to serve as Vice-Chancellor of a British university (University of London).
5th - 13th	The first Aldeburgh Festival takes place in the Aldeburgh area of Suffolk. Founded by the composer Benjamin Britten the arts festival is devoted mainly to classical music.
21st	The Manchester Small-Scale Experimental Machine, the world's first stored-program computer, runs its first program. Nicknamed Baby it was built at the Victoria University of Manchester by Frederic C. Williams, Tom Kilburn and Geoff Tootill.
21st	Sir Ernest Beachcroft Beckwith Towse (born 23rd April 1864) dies. When Towse was 35 years old he was awarded the Victoria Cross whilst serving as a captain in the 1st Battalion, The Gordon Highlanders during the Second Boer War. The War Office awarded Towse with a special wounds pension of £300 a year which was possibly at the insistence of Queen Victoria who is said to have shed tears when pinning the decoration to him.

22nd June: The passenger liner Empire Windrush arrives in Britain bringing one of the first large groups of post-war West Indian immigrants to the UK. The ship was carrying 492 passengers and one stowaway on the voyage from Jamaica to London. This voyage led to British Caribbean people who came to the UK after World War II sometimes being referred to as the Windrush generation.

JUNE

22nd   In recognising the independence of India in 1947 an Order in Council removes the title of Emperor of India from the Royal Style and Titles.

28th   The British begin airlift Operation Plainfare to West Berlin in response to the Berlin Blockade.

The Berlin Blockade was one of the first major international crises of the Cold War. During the multinational occupation of post–World War II Germany, the Soviet Union blocked the Western Allies' railway, road and canal access to the sectors of Berlin under Western control. In response, the Allies organised the Berlin airlift to carry supplies to the people of West Berlin. Aircrews from the United States, Britain, Canada, Australia, New Zealand and South Africa flew over 200,000 flights in one year, providing to the West Berliners up to 8,893 tons of necessities each day. By the spring of 1949 the airlift was clearly succeeding and by April it was delivering more cargo than had previously been transported into the city by rail. On the 12th May 1949 the USSR lifted the blockade of West Berlin.

JULY

1st   The Town and Country Planning Act of 1947 (and its equivalent in Scotland) comes into effect. As the foundation of modern town and country planning it requires planning permission for land development and establishes the system of Listed buildings.

1st   The National Museum of Wales opens the Welsh Folk Museum at St Fagans to the public. It is the first open-air museum in the UK and chronicles the historical lifestyle, culture and architecture of the Welsh people.

4th   A Scandinavian Airlines Douglas DC-6 and an Avro York of No. 99 Squadron RAF collide over Northwood, London. The crash kills all 39 people aboard both aircraft.

JULY

5th	The National Health Service begins functioning and gives the right to universal free healthcare at the point of use.
5th	The Children Act 1948 comes into effect. It transfers responsibility for child welfare from Poor Law Guardians, Approved Schools and voluntary organisations to new local authority Children's Departments with professional Children's Officers.
14th	Six Vampire F.3 aircraft of No.54 Squadron RAF become the first jet aircraft to fly across the Atlantic Ocean.
15th	The first London chapter of Alcoholics Anonymous is founded.
25th	Post-War bread rationing ends.
29th - 14th Aug	The Olympic Games are held in London and are opened by King George VI.
29th	The Stoke Mandeville Games are held for the first time. These are the predecessor of the modern Paralympic Games.
29th	The highest recorded Central England temperature reaches 25.2°C (77.4°F).
30th	1,064 privately owned and municipal gas companies are merged into twelve area Gas Boards as the government nationalises the gas industry.

John Mark holds the Olympic Flame aloft at the opening ceremony of the XIV Olympiad.

After a 12-year hiatus because of World War II these were the first Summer Olympics since the 1936 Games in Berlin. Great Britain and Northern Ireland would win 3 gold, 14 silver and 6 bronze medals at the games which are televised by the BBC. In total 4,104 athletes competed in 136 events over 19 sporting disciplines. Germany and Japan were refused permission to participate in the games and although the USSR was invited they chose not to send any athletes. This was the second occasion that London had hosted the Olympic Games having previously held them in 1908. The Olympics again returned to London in 2012 making it thus far the only city to have hosted the games three times.

AUGUST

12th	The inventor of rustless steel (now known as stainless steel) Harry Brearley (born 18th February 1871) dies.

AUGUST

18th — Jockey Lester Piggott, aged just 12 years old, wins his first race on a horse called The Chase at Haydock Park. Piggott goes on to have 4,493 career wins (including nine Epsom Derby victories) and is widely regarded as one of the greatest flat racing jockeys of all time.

SEPTEMBER

The first new comprehensive schools open in Potters Bar and Hillingdon.

Judicial corporal punishment (birching and flogging) is abolished in the UK. It continues to persist in prisons as a punishment for prisoners committing serious assaults on prison staff until the advent of the Criminal Justice Act 1967.

6th — Flying the de Havilland DH 108, Squadron Leader John Derry becomes the first British pilot to break the sound barrier. Derry is killed four years later, aged 30, at the 1952 Farnborough Airshow when his aircraft breaks up because of a design fault. The catastrophic structural failure leads to 31 fatalities including himself, his flight observer Tony Richards and 29 spectators.

8th — Terence Rattigan's play, The Browning Version, premieres at the Phoenix Theatre in London.

OCTOBER

The 1948 Earls Court Motor Show.

27th October - 6th November: The first post-war Motor Show is held at Earls Court, London. A record 562,954 visitors witness a wide range of new products from British manufacturers including the Jaguar XK120 (which at the time is the world's fastest production car). The most successful of those on display will be the Morris Minor and Land Rover.

October

6th
The Hoover Company opens a new factory for the mass production of washing machines at Merthyr Tydfil.
Paleoanthropologist Mary Leakey finds the first partial fossilised skull of Proconsul Africanus (an ancestor of apes and humans) on Rusinga Island in Kenya.

12th
Topical debate programme Any Questions? is broadcast for the first time on the BBC Home Service. It is still being broadcast today.

20th
A KLM Lockheed Constellation airliner crashes into power cables on approach to Prestwick Airport killing all 40 people on board.

November

8th
King George VI issues Letters Patent granting the title of Prince or Princess of the United Kingdom, with the style Royal Highness, to the children of The Duke of Edinburgh and The Princess Elizabeth, Duchess of Edinburgh.

14th
Princess Elizabeth gives birth to a son.

15th
Rising actor and comedian Ronnie Barker, aged 19, makes his stage debut in the play Quality Street at the County Theatre in Aylesbury, Buckinghamshire.

December

Patrick Blackett wins the Nobel Prize in Physics for 'his development of the Wilson cloud chamber method and his discoveries therewith in the fields of nuclear physics and cosmic radiation'.
American-born British poet T.S. Eliot wins the Nobel Prize in Literature for 'his outstanding pioneer contribution to present-day poetry'.

15th
The Duke and Duchess of Edinburgh's one-month-old child is christened His Royal Highness Charles Philip Arthur George of Edinburgh. Charles was created Prince of Wales and Earl of Chester on the 26th July 1958 although his investiture as Prince of Wales was not conducted until the 1st July 1969 when he was crowned by his mother in a televised ceremony held at Caernarfon Castle.

26th
The first series of Reith Lectures featuring Bertrand Russell on 'Authority and the Individual' are broadcast on the BBC Home Service. Still going today the 2016 Reith Lectures featured Stephen Hawking on 'Do Black Holes Have No Hair?'

31st
Sir Malcolm Campbell (born 11th March 1885) dies aged 63. The racing motorist and motoring journalist achieved the world speed records on land and on water at various times during the 1920s and 1930s.

Undated Events from 1948

- Scottish advocate Margaret Kidd becomes the first British woman King's Counsel in Britain.
- The Snettisham Hoard discovered near King's Lynn.
- The National Youth Orchestra of Great Britain is founded by Ruth Railton.

10 Noteable Worldwide Events

1. 30th January - Mahatma Gandhi is assassinated in New Delhi by Hindu militant Nathuram Godse.
2. 7th April - The World Health Organization is established by the United Nations.
3. Georges de Mestral, an engineer from Switzerland, first starts his work on inventing hook and loop fasteners. By 1955 he had successfully patented his idea and named his invention Velcro (formed from the two French words: velours for velvet and crochet for hook).
4. 18th June - Columbia Records unveil the LP record at a New York press conference. Developed by Peter Goldmark of CBS Laboratories the LP is a 12-inch (30 cm) Long Play (LP) 33 1/3 rpm microgroove record album. 1949 sees RCA Victor follow this with the first 45 rpm single which measures 7 inches in diameter.
5. Bertram Forer demonstrates the Forer effect in that people tend to accept generalised descriptions of personality as uniquely applicable to themselves.
6. John and Margaret Walson create the first cable television company when they form Service Electric Cable Television in the mountains of Pennsylvania in 1948.
7. 20-year-old Newman Darby invents windsurfing. In 1948 he was the first to conceive the idea of using a handheld sail and rig mounted on a universal joint so that he could control his small catamaran - the first rudderless sailboard ever built that allowed a person to steer by shifting his or her weight in order to tilt the sail fore and aft.
8. Designed and built by the Wright brothers in 1903 the Wright Flyer, the first powered heavier-than-air machine to achieve controlled sustained flight with a pilot, goes on display in the Smithsonian.
9. 20th November - The Takahē, a flightless bird generally thought to have been extinct for fifty years, is rediscovered by Geoffrey Orbell near Lake Te Anau on the South Island of New Zealand.
10. 10th December - The Universal Declaration of Human Rights (UDHR) is adopted by the United Nations General Assembly at the Palais de Chaillot in Paris.

Orville Wright at the controls of the 'Wright Flyer' as his brother Wilbur Wright looks on during the plane's first flight at Kitty Hawk, North Carolina, United States on the 17th December 1903.

U.K. Personalities Born in 1948

Anthony Colin Gerald Andrews
12th January 1948

Actor best known for his award winning role as Lord Sebastian Flyte in the 1981 ITV miniseries Brideshead Revisited (he was the winner of a Golden Globe and BAFTA TV Award). On stage Andrews has played Professor Higgins in My Fair Lady and Count Fosco in Andrew Lloyd Webber's The Woman in White. Notable films include Ivanhoe (1982), The Scarlet Pimpernel (1982) and the King's Speech (2010).

Malcolm J. 'Mal' Reilly
19th January 1948

Rugby league footballer and coach. At club level for he played for Castleford and Manly-Warringah (in Australia) between 1967 and 1986. He also represented England and Great Britain during this time. Reilly's coaching career including being appointed head coach of Great Britain from 1987 until 1994 when he stood down. In 2014 he was inaugurated into the British Rugby League Hall of Fame.

Anthony Frank 'Tony' Iommi
19th February 1948

Guitarist, songwriter and producer best known as the lead guitarist (and one of the four founding members) of the heavy metal band Black Sabbath. Iommi has been the band's sole continual member and primary composer for nearly five decades. Sabbath have sold over 70 million records worldwide and were inducted into the UK Music Hall of Fame in 2005 and the Rock and Roll Hall of Fame in 2006. They also have two Grammy Awards for Best Metal Performance.

Andrew Lloyd Webber, Baron Lloyd-Webber
22nd March 1948

Composer and impresario of musical theatre. Several of his musicals have run for more than a decade in the West End and on Broadway and he has received numerous awards including 7 Tonys, 3 Grammys, an Academy Award, 14 Ivor Novello Awards, 7 Olivier Awards, a Golden Globe and the 2008 Classic Brit Award for Outstanding Contribution to Music. He is an inductee into the Songwriter's Hall of Fame and is a fellow of the British Academy of Songwriters, Composers and Authors.

Derek Thompson
4th April 1948

Northern Irish actor most notable for playing Charlie Fairhead in the long-running BBC television medical drama series Casualty. Thompson has played the role since the series' inception in 1986. Before appearing in Casualty he had a recurring role as DS Jimmy Fenton in the ITV police drama The Gentle Touch. He has also had minor film roles in Yanks (1979) and Breaking Glass (1980), and also played Jeff, Harold Shand's lieutenant, in The Long Good Friday (1980).

Jeremy James Anthony Gibson-Beadle, MBE
12th April 1948 -
30th January 2008

Television and radio presenter, writer and producer. During the 1980s he was a regular face on British television and his shows regularly topped the television charts. He was also the first mainstream television presenter to have a physical disability. Beadle was made a Member of the Order of the British Empire (MBE) for his services to charity in the 2001 New Year Honours (his total charitable fund raising is estimated to be in the order of £100 million).

Sir Terence David John 'Terry' Pratchett, OBE
28th April 1948 -
12th March 2015

Author of fantasy novels who is best known for his Discworld series of 41 novels. Pratchett's first novel, The Carpet People, was published in 1971 and the first Discworld novel, The Colour of Magic, was published in 1983 (after which he wrote two books a year on average). Pratchett has sold more than 85 million books, in 37 languages, throughout his career and was one of the UK's best-selling authors of the 1990s.

Pamela E. 'Pam' Ferris
11th May 1948

Welsh actress whose popular television roles include Ma Larkin in The Darling Buds of May, Peggy Snow in Where The Heart Is, Laura Thyme in Rosemary & Thyme, Catherina 'Cath' Smith in Gavin & Stacey and Sister Evangelina in Call The Midwife. Ferris has also played parts in a number of films such as Miss Trunchbull in Matilda (1996) and as Aunt Marge in Harry Potter And The Prisoner of Azkaban (2004).

Robert 'Bob' Champion, MBE
4th June 1948

Former jump jockey who won the 1981 Grand National on Aldaniti. His triumph was made into the film Champions (1984) with John Hurt portraying Champion. He was appointed Member of the Order of the British Empire in the 1982 Queen's Birthday Honours and in 2011 Champion received the Helen Rollason Award as part of the BBC Sports Personality Of The Year competition.

Ian Russell McEwan, CBE FRSA FRSL
21st June 1948

Novelist and screenwriter who won the 1998 Man Booker Prize with Amsterdam. His follow up novel Atonement was adapted into an Oscar-winning film starring Keira Knightley and James McAvoy. In 2008 The Times featured him on their list of The 50 Greatest British Writers Since 1945, and The Daily Telegraph ranked him number 19 in their list of the '100 most powerful people in British culture'. In 2011 he was awarded the Jerusalem Prize which is given to writers whose works have dealt with themes of human freedom in society.

Yusuf Islam
21st July 1948

Folk singer-songwriter, multi-instrumentalist, humanitarian and education philanthropist, who is more commonly known by his former stage name Cat Stevens. His 1967 debut album reached the top 10 in the UK and the album's title song Matthew And Son' charted at No.2. His albums Tea for the Tillerman (1970) and Teaser And The Firecat (1971) were both certified triple platinum in the US. In 2007 he received the British Academy's Ivor Novello Award for Outstanding Song Collection.

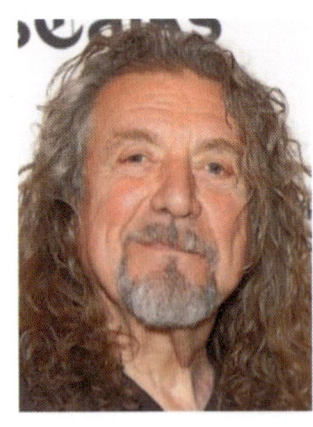

Robert Plant, CBE
20th August 1948

Iconic rock star who gained fame as the vocalist and songwriter of the classic rock band Led Zeppelin. Plant is regarded as one of the greatest singers in the history of rock and roll and was named the No.1 Lead Singer of All Time by Rolling Stone Magazine in 2011. Led Zeppelin are one of the best-selling music groups in the history of audio recording with estimated record sales of 200 to 300 million units worldwide.

Julia Catherine Donaldson, MBE
16th September 1948

Writer, playwright, performer and the 2011-2013 Children's Laureate. She is best known for her popular rhyming stories for children, especially those illustrated by Axel Scheffler, which include The Gruffalo, Room on the Broom and Stick Man. Donaldson has 184 published works of which 64 are widely available in bookshops. The remaining 120 are intended for school use and include her Songbirds phonic reading scheme, which is part of the Oxford Reading Tree.

Jeremy John Irons
19th September 1948

Actor who began his acting career on stage in 1969. He has since appeared in many West End theatre productions and in 1984 made his Broadway debut in Tom Stoppard's The Real Thing. Irons' first major film role came in the 1981 romantic drama The French Lieutenant's Woman. He is one of the few actors who have won the 'Triple Crown of Acting' - winning an Academy Award, an Emmy Award and a Tony Award. In October 2011 he was nominated Goodwill Ambassador of the Food and Agriculture Organization of the United Nations.

Olivia Newton-John, AO, OBE
26th September 1948

British-Australian singer, songwriter and actress who is a four-time Grammy award winner. With a hugely successful music career behind her Newton-John has sold an estimated 100 million records worldwide making her one of the world's best-selling music artists of all time. As an actress she is probably best remembered for playing the part of Sandy in Grease (1978) which featured one of the most successful soundtracks in Hollywood history.

Michele Dotrice
27th September 1948

Actress, best known for her portrayal of Betty Spencer, the long-suffering wife of Frank Spencer, in the BBC sitcom Some Mothers Do 'Ave 'Em (1973-1978). Since then she has made numerous guest appearances in well-known British television series and the mid-1990s saw her appearing in several episodes of the period drama Bramwell. More recently, in 2016, she played Nancy the faithful dresser and woman of all work to the main character in the West End production of Nell Gwynn.

Gerard 'Gerry' Adams
6th October 1948

Irish republican politician who is the president of the Sinn Féin political party and a Teachta Dála for Louth since the 2011 general election. From 1983-1992 and from 1997-2011 he was an abstentionist MP of the British Parliament for the Belfast West constituency. He has been the president of Sinn Féin since 1983 and since that time the party has become the third-largest party in the Republic of Ireland and the second-largest political party in Northern Ireland.

Richard John 'Rick' Parfitt, OBE
12th October 1948 - 24th December 2016

Musician who is best known as a singer, songwriter and rhythm guitarist for rock band Status Quo. Parfitt's almost 50-year career with the band began in 1967. Status Quo's popularity grew in the 1970s with songs such as Paper Plane, Caroline, Down Down, Rockin' All Over the World and Whatever You Want. To date the band has sold over 118 million records worldwide and in 1991 received a Brit Award for Outstanding Contribution to Music. Parfitt was appointed an OBE in 2010 alongside fellow band member Francis Rossi.

Christopher John Davison
15th October 1948

Singer, songwriter and instrumentalist better known professionally as Chris de Burgh. He has had several top 40 hits in the UK and two in the US but is more popular in other countries, particularly Norway and Brazil. He is probably most famous for his 1986 love song 'The Lady In Red' which reached number one in several countries. De Burgh has sold over 45 million albums worldwide and although signed to A&M Records for many years he now has his own label, Ferryman Productions.

Lulu Kennedy-Cairns, OBE
3rd November 1948

Scottish singer songwriter, actress, television personality and businesswoman who was born Marie McDonald McLaughlin Lawrie but is better known by her stage name Lulu. Her first hit Shout reached No.7 in the UK charts in 1964 and her highest UK charting single was the Eurovision Song Contest winning entry, Boom Bang-a-Bang, at No.2. She is internationally identified with the song To Sir With Love and with the title song to the James Bond film The Man With The Golden Gun.

Charles, Prince of Wales (Charles Philip Arthur George)
14th November 1948

Heir apparent known alternatively in South West England as Duke of Cornwall and in Scotland as Duke of Rothesay. He is the longest-serving heir apparent in British history, having held the position since 1952, and is also the oldest person to be next in line to the throne since Sophia of Hanover who died in 1714 at the age of 83. Charles's interests encompass a range of humanitarian and social issues leading him to found The Prince's Trust in 1976 (to help build the confidence and motivation of disadvantaged young people).

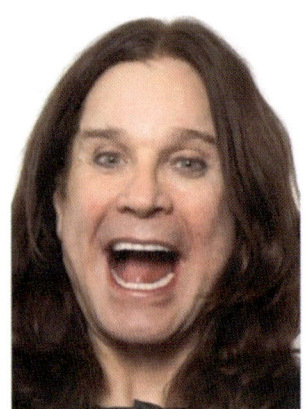

John Michael 'Ozzy' Osbourne
3rd December 1948

Singer, songwriter and actor who rose to prominence in the early 1970s as the lead vocalist of heavy metal band Black Sabbath. After he was fired from the band in 1979 he went on to have a successful solo career with several multi-platinum albums in the US. He has reunited with Black Sabbath on several occasions and has been inducted into the UK Music Hall of Fame as a solo artist and as a member of the band. Osbourne is often referred to as the Prince of Darkness and the Godfather of Heavy Metal.

Peter David Robinson
29th December 1948

Former Northern Irish politician and Leader of the Democratic Unionist Party (DUP) who was First Minister of Northern Ireland from 2008 until his retirement in 2016. He has been involved in Northern Irish politics for over 40 years and in 1979 became the youngest-serving Member of Parliament (MP) when he was narrowly elected for Belfast East. He held this seat until his defeat by Naomi Long in 2010 making him the longest-serving Belfast MP since the 1800 Act of Union.

POPULAR MUSIC 1948

```
No.1    Dinah Shore           Buttons & Bows
No.2    Pee Wee Hunt          12th Street Rag
No.3    Nat King Cole         Nature Boy
No.4    The Andrews Sisters   Near You
No.5    Kay Kyser             The Woody Woodpecker Song
No.6    Peggy Lee             Mañana (Is Soon Enough For Me)
No.7    Bing Crosby           Now Is The Hour
No.8    Doris Day             It's Magic
No.9    Gracie Fields         Now Is The Hour
No.10   Spike Jones           All I Want For Christmas Is My
                              Two Front Teeth
```

Dinah Shore
Buttons & Bows

Label:
Columbia (D.B. 2446)

Written by:
Jay Livingston / Raymond Evans

Length:
2 mins 4 secs

Dinah Shore (born Frances Rose Shore; 29th February 1916 - 24th February 1994) was a singer, actress, television personality and the top-charting female vocalist during the Big Band era of the 1940s and 1950s. After failing singing auditions for Benny Goodman, Jimmy Dorsey and his brother Tommy Dorsey, Shore struck out on her own achieving huge solo success.

Pee Wee Hunt
12th Street Rag

Label:
Capitol Records (CL 13002)

Written by:
Euday Bowman / James Sumner

Length:
2 mins 46 secs

Pee Wee Hunt (born Walter Gerhardt Hunt; 10th May 1907 - 22nd June 1979) was a jazz trombonist, vocalist and band leader. His 'Twelfth Street Rag' was a No.1 hit in September 1948 and sold over three million records.

Nat King Cole
Nature Boy

Label:
Capitol Records (15054)

Written by:
Eden Ahbez

Length:
2 mins 50 secs

Nathaniel Adams Coles (17th March 1919 - 15th February 1965), known professionally as Nat King Cole, was a singer who first came to prominence as a leading jazz pianist. He was widely noted for his soft baritone voice performing in big band and jazz genres. Cole was one of the first African Americans to host a national television variety show, The Nat King Cole Show.

The Andrews Sisters
Near You

Label:
Decca (74021)

Written by:
Francis Craig / Kermit Goell

Length:
3 mins 2 secs

The Andrews Sisters were a close harmony singing group from the eras of swing and boogie-woogie. The group consisted of three sisters: LaVerne Sophia (6th July 1911 - 8th May 1967), Maxene Angelyn (3rd January 1916 - 21st October 1995) and Patricia Marie (16th February 1918 - 30th January 2013). Throughout their long career the sisters sold over 75 million records.

 ## Kay Kyser
The Woody Woodpecker Song

Label:
V Disc (849)

Written by:
George Tibbles / Ramey Idriss

Length:
3 mins 9 secs

James Kern 'Kay' Kyser (18th June 1905 - 23rd July 1985) was an American bandleader and radio personality of the 1930s and 1940s. The Woody Wood Pecker Song (sung by Gloria Wood) received an Oscar nomination for the best song in 1949 and remained at No.1 in the charts for six weeks.

 ## Peggy Lee
Mañana (Is Soon Enough For Me)

Label:
Capitol Records (15022)

Written by:
Dave Barbour / Peggy Lee

Length:
2 mins 53 secs

Peggy Lee (born Norma Deloris Egstrom; 26th May 1920 - 21st January 2002) was a jazz and popular music singer, songwriter, composer and actress. In a career spanning six decades this recording of Mañana (backed by Dave Barbour's Orchestra) became her biggest charting hit. Lee was a recipient of three Grammy Awards and an inductee of the Songwriters Hall Of Fame (1999).

Bing Crosby
Now Is The Hour

Label: Decca (L 4541)

Written by: Scott / Stewart / Kaihan

Length: 3 mins 10 secs

Harry Lillis 'Bing' Crosby, Jr. (3rd May 1903 - 14th October 1977) was a singer and actor. Crosby's trademark warm bass-baritone voice made him the best-selling recording artist of the 20th century selling close to a billion records, tapes, compact discs and digital downloads worldwide.

Doris Day
It's Magic

Label: Columbia (38188)

Written by: Jule Styne / Sammy Cahn

Length: 3 mins 5 secs

Doris Day (born Doris Mary Ann Kappelhoff; 3rd April 1922) is a retired actress and singer, and continuing animal welfare activist. It's Magic was introduced by Doris Day in her 1948 film debut, Romance on the High Seas (known in the UK as It's Magic after the song).

⑨ Gracie Fields
Now Is The Hour

Label:
London Records (DR.11487)

Written by:
Scott / Stewart / Kaihan

Length:
3 mins 7 secs

Dame Gracie Fields, DBE (born Grace Stansfield; 9th January 1898 - 27th September 1979) was an actress, singer, comedian, and a star of both cinema and music hall. The song Now Is The Hour achieved world-wide popularity in 1948 with no less than seven charting recordings (including that of Bing Crosby).

⑩ Spike Jones (And His City Slickers)
All I Want For Christmas Is My Two Front Teeth

Label:
RCA Victor (20-3177)

Written by:
Donald Gardner

Length:
2 mins 21 secs

Lindley Armstrong 'Spike' Jones (14th December 1911 - 1st May 1965) was a musician and bandleader specialising in satirical arrangements of popular songs. Ballads and classical works receiving the Jones treatment were punctuated with gunshots, whistles, cowbells and outlandish vocals. All I Want For Christmas Is My Two Front Teeth (with vocals by George Rock) was Jones' only No.1 record.

TOP FILMS 1948

1. The Red Shoes
2. The Three Musketeers
3. Red River
4. The Treasure Of The Sierra Madre
5. Easter Parade

OSCARS

Best Film: Hamlet

Best Director: John Huston
(*The Treasure Of The Sierra Madre*)
Best Actor: Laurence Olivier
(*Hamlet*)
Best Actress: Jane Wyman
(*Johnny Belinda*)
Best Supporting Actor: Walter Huston
(*The Treasure Of The Sierra Madre*)
Best Supporting Actress: Claire Trevor
(*Key Largo*)

THE RED SHOES

Directed by: Michael Powell & Emeric Pressburger - Runtime: 134 minutes

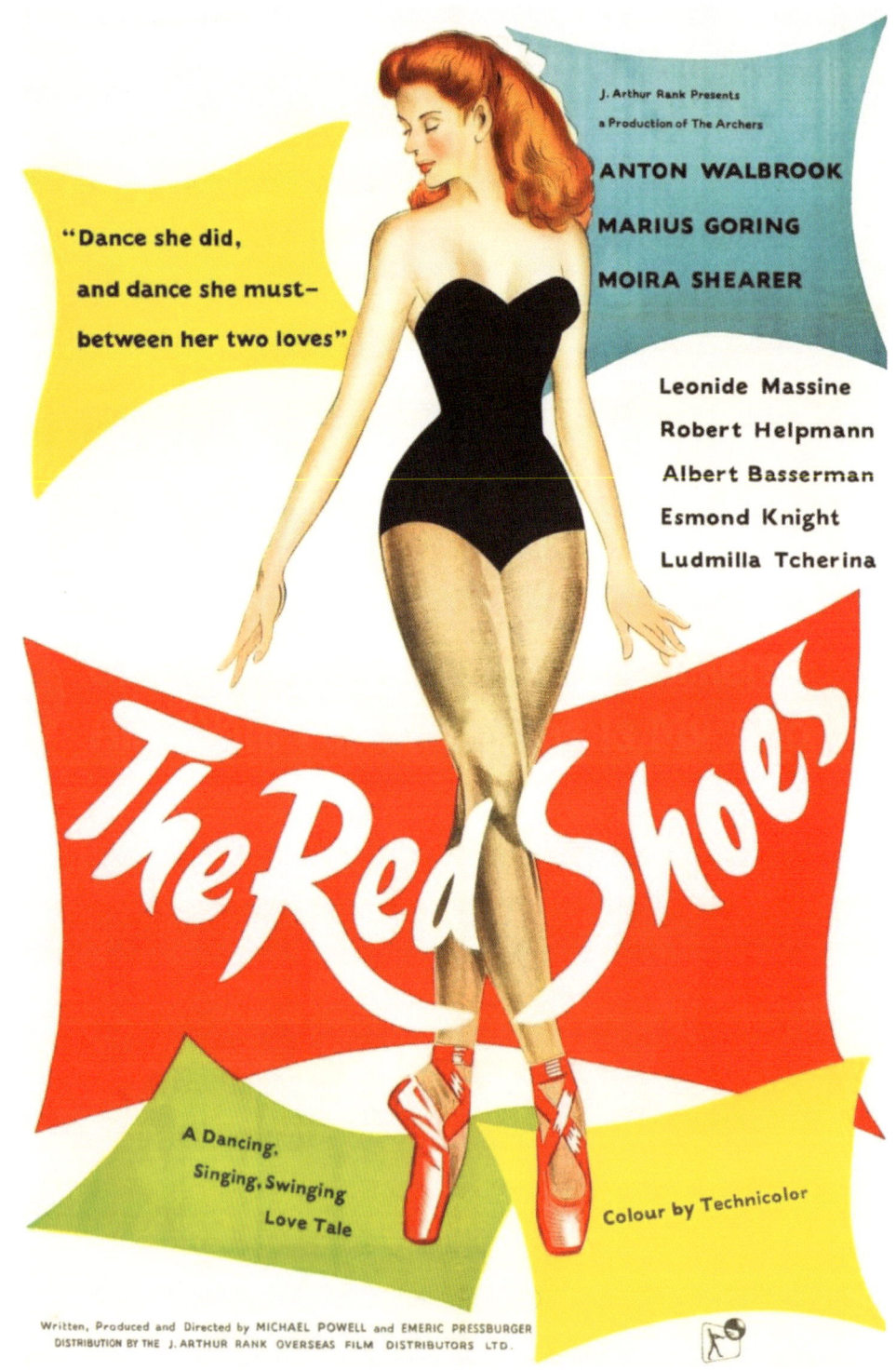

Young ballerina Victoria Page is poised for superstardom but is torn between the man she loves and her pursuit to become a prima ballerina.

STARRING

Anton Walbrook
Born: 19th November 1896
Died: 9th August 1967

Character:
Boris Lermontov

Adolf Anton Wilhelm Wohlbrück was an Austrian actor who settled in the United Kingdom under the name Anton Walbrook. He was descended from ten generations of actors although his father broke with tradition and was a circus clown. Walbrook studied with the director Max Reinhardt and built up a career in Austrian theatre and cinema before going to Hollywood in 1936. His last film was I accuse! (1958).

Marius Goring, CBE
Born: 23rd May 1912
Died: 30th September 1998

Character:
Julian Craster

An English stage and film actor who is most often remembered for the four films he made with Powell & Pressburger, particularly as Conductor 71 in A Matter Of Life And Death (1946). Goring was fluent in both French and German and regularly performed French and German roles. He was made a Fellow of the Royal Society of Literature in 1979 and appointed Commander of the Order of the British Empire (CBE) in 1991.

Moira Shearer
Born: 17th January 1926
Died: 31st January 2006

Character:
Victoria Page

An actress and internationally renowned ballet dancer who came to international attention for her first film role as Victoria Page in The Red Shoes. Although she went on to star in other films and worked as a dancer for many decades, she is primarily known for playing 'Vicky'. Shearer also wrote for The Daily Telegraph newspaper and gave talks on ballet worldwide.

TRIVIA

Goofs   Just before Julian Craster begins to play the piano for the first time for Lermontov the shadow of a boom mic can be seen moving into position, projected against the wall behind him.

When Vicky begins to dance with the newspaper character only the words 'Le Journal' are typed across his face. Partway through the dance his face is covered with newsprint.

Interesting Facts   Jack Cardiff deliberately manipulated camera speed during the Red Shoes ballet to create the effect of dancers almost hovering in mid-air at the peak of their jumps.

CONTINUED

Interesting Facts

When Ludovic Kennedy saw Moira Shearer in this film he said that he knew instantly that she was going to be the girl he would marry. He actively sought her out and married her two years later in the Chapel Royal in London's Hampton Court Palace.

Casting the role of Vicky Page was a tough call for Michael Powell and Emeric Pressburger. Ideally they wanted a ballerina who could act and who also had to be ravishingly beautiful. They were thrilled when they discovered Moira Shearer, who was second to Margot Fonteyn at the famous Sadler's Wells Ballet, but she initially rebuffed them. It took them a year to persuade her to change her mind.

The Red Shoes was nominated for 5 Academy Awards winning two, Best Original Score and Best Art Direction.

A restored print has been made by Martin Scorsese's Film Foundation and the UCLA Film & Television Archive, after many years work. The restorers went right back to the original negatives, digitally repairing any scratches and misalignment. The restored print was shown at Cannes in 2009 to great acclaim.

Quote

Boris Lermontov: Why do you want to dance?
([Vicky thinks for a short while]
Victoria Page: Why do you want to live?
[Lermontov is surprised at the answer]
Boris Lermontov: Well I don't know exactly why, er, but I must.
Victoria Page: That's my answer too.

THE THREE MUSKETEERS

Directed by: George Sidney - Runtime: 125 minutes

D'Artagnan and his musketeer comrades, Athos, Porthos and Aramis, thwart the plans of Royal Prime Minister Richelieu to usurp the King's power.

STARRING

Lana Turner
Born: 8th February 1921
Died: 29th June 1995

Character:
Lady de Winter

Film and television actress who was discovered in 1937 and signed by Metro-Goldwyn-Mayer aged just 16. Turner first attracted attention in They Won't Forget (1937). During the early 1940s she established herself as a leading actress and her popularity continued during the 1950s with films such as Peyton Place (1957) for which she was nominated for an Academy Award for Best Actress.

Gene Kelly
Born: 23rd August 1912
Died: 2nd February 1996

Character:
D'Artagnan

Dancer, actor, singer, film director, producer and choreographer. He is best known today for his performances in films such as An American In Paris (1951), Anchors Aweigh (1945) and Singin' In The Rain (1952). Kelly received an Academy Honorary Award in 1952 for his career achievements and in 1999 the American Film Institute put him at 15th in their Greatest Male Stars of Classic Hollywood cinema list.

June Allyson
Born: 7th October 1917
Died: 8th July 2006

Character:
Constance

Stage, film and television actress, dancer, and singer, born Eleanor Geisman. She began her career as a dancer in short subject films in 1937 and in 1938 on Broadway. She signed with MGM in 1943 and rose to fame the following year in the musical Two Girls and a Sailor (1944). In 1951 she won the Golden Globe Award for Best Actress for her performance in the romantic comedy film Too Young to Kiss.

TRIVIA

Goofs

During the first sword fight scene Gascon splashes water out of a bird bath into his opponent's face. After the fight the musketeers walk away laughing and the camera overhead shot reveals that the bird bath is completely dry.

Near the end of the movie D'Artagnan removes and drops his hat as he leaps into the water from the castle parapet. Seconds later he is riding at full gallop with his hat on.

The storyline for the film takes place in 1625 yet shows King Louis XIII as an old man. In reality Louis (1601 to 1643) would have only been 24 years old at the time.

CONTINUED

Interesting Facts Lana Turner originally accepted a studio suspension in preference to playing Lady de Winter because she considered her a secondary character.

Thirty-five year old Gene Kelly's character D'Artagnan was supposed to be nineteen at the beginning of the film.

Lana Turner was ordered to lose weight before filming began in what would be her first appearance in a colour feature film.

Fearing pressure from church groups MGM had the script refer to Richelieu as Prime Minister rather than Cardinal. Almost all traces of him being a cardinal or a man of the church were removed.

Quotes **Constance Bonacieux:** Oh monsieur! Monsieur, you come from the heavens.
D'Artagnan: No mademoiselle, just from upstairs.

Athos: To die among friends. Can a man ask more? Can the world offer less? Who wants to live 'till the last bottle is empty? It's all-for one, d'Artagnan, and one for all.

RED RIVER

Directed by: Howard Hawks & Arthur Rosson - Runtime: 92 minutes

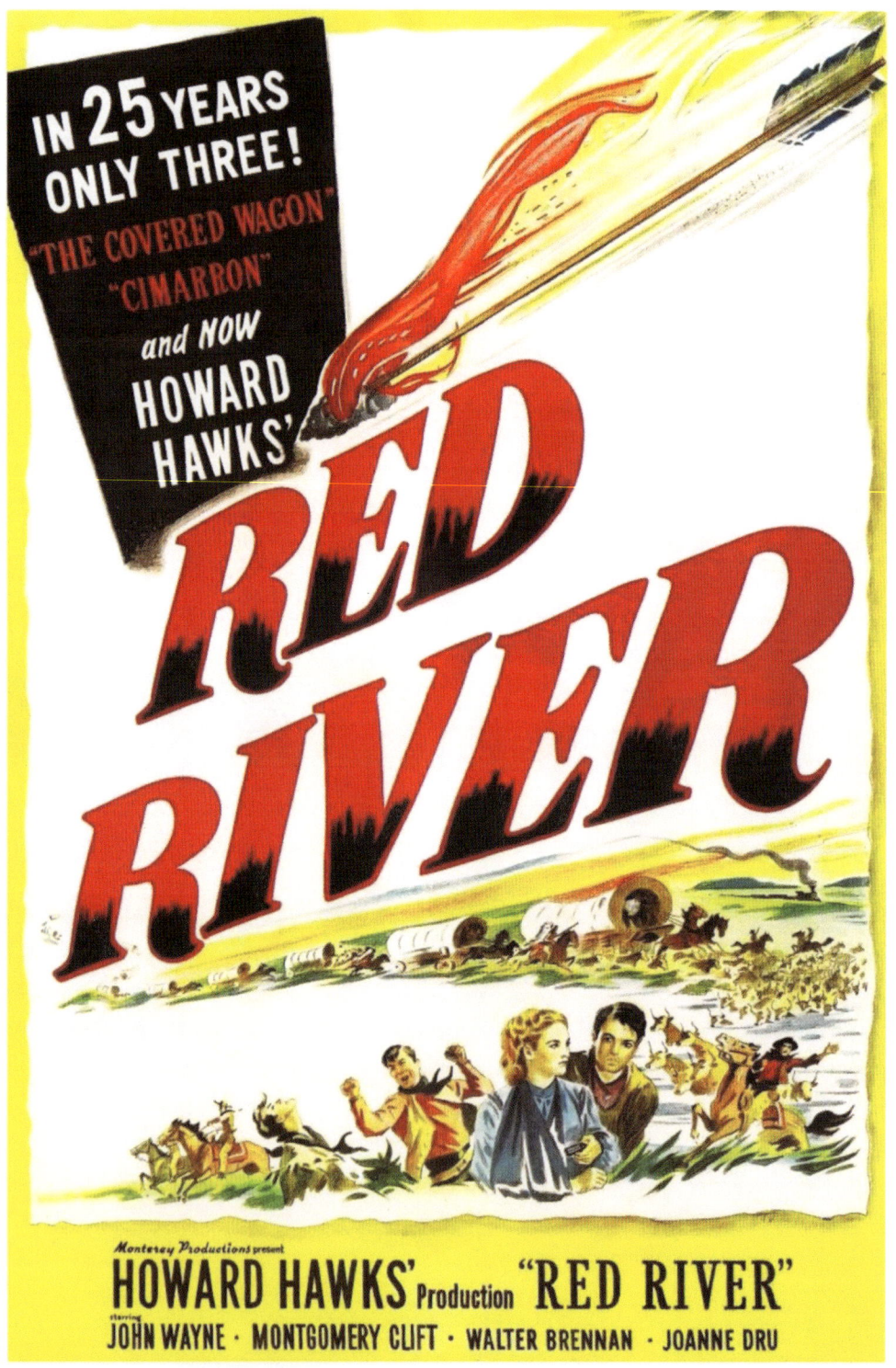

Tom Dunson leads a cattle drive to its destination 1,000 miles away in Missouri but his tyrannical behaviour along the way causes a mutiny, led by his adopted son Matt Garth.

STARRING

John Wayne
Born: 26th May 1907
Died: 11th June 1979

Character:
Thomas Dunson

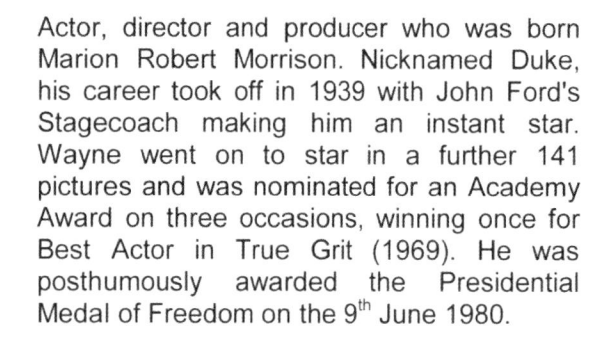

Actor, director and producer who was born Marion Robert Morrison. Nicknamed Duke, his career took off in 1939 with John Ford's Stagecoach making him an instant star. Wayne went on to star in a further 141 pictures and was nominated for an Academy Award on three occasions, winning once for Best Actor in True Grit (1969). He was posthumously awarded the Presidential Medal of Freedom on the 9th June 1980.

Montgomery Clift
Born: 17th October 1920
Died: 23rd July 1966

Character:
Matt Garth

Film and stage actor who is best remembered for his roles in Red River (1948), The Heiress (1949), A Place in the Sun (1951), I Confess (1952), From Here to Eternity (1953) and Judgment at Nuremberg (1961). Along with Marlon Brando and James Dean, Clift was one of the original method actors in Hollywood. He received four Academy Award nominations during his career, three for Best Actor and one for Best Supporting Actor.

Joanne Dru
Born: 31st January 1922
Died: 10th September 1996

Character:
Tess Millay

Film and television actress best known for films such as Red River, All the King's Men (1949) and The Pride of St. Louis (1952). Her film career petered out by the end of the 1950s but she continued working frequently in television, most notably as Babs Wooten on the 1960-61 sitcom Guestward, Ho!. For her contribution to the television industry Dru was awarded a star on the Hollywood Walk of Fame on the 8th February 1960.

TRIVIA

Goofs

The film is set in 1865 yet several 1873 Colt Single-Action Army Revolvers and 1892 Winchesters are seen throughout the film.

During the cattle stampede Dunson, Matt and the other cowboys saddle up and try to turn the herd. Process shots of each cowboy are inserted in the scene. Every cowboy is riding the same dummy horse and saddle with a very large Mexican saddlehorn.

At the end of the film when Dunson finally confronts Matt and after knocking Matt down twice, Matt punches back knocking Dunson's hat off. The very next punch from Matt knocks Dunson's hat off again.

CONTINUED

Interesting Facts After seeing John Wayne's performance in Red River, directed by rival director Howard Hawks, John Ford is quoted as saying, 'I never knew the big son of a bitch could act.' This led to Ford casting Wayne in more complex roles in films such as She Wore a Yellow Ribbon (1949) and The Searchers (1956).

Texas Longhorn cattle had been virtually extinct for about 50 years when this film was made and only a few dozen animals were available. In the herd scenes most of the cattle are Hereford crosses with the precious Longhorns being prominently placed during crucial scenes.

In an interview with Life Magazine, John Wayne described Montgomery Clift as 'an arrogant little bastard'.

The Treasure Of The Sierra Madre

Directed by: John Huston - Runtime: 126 minutes

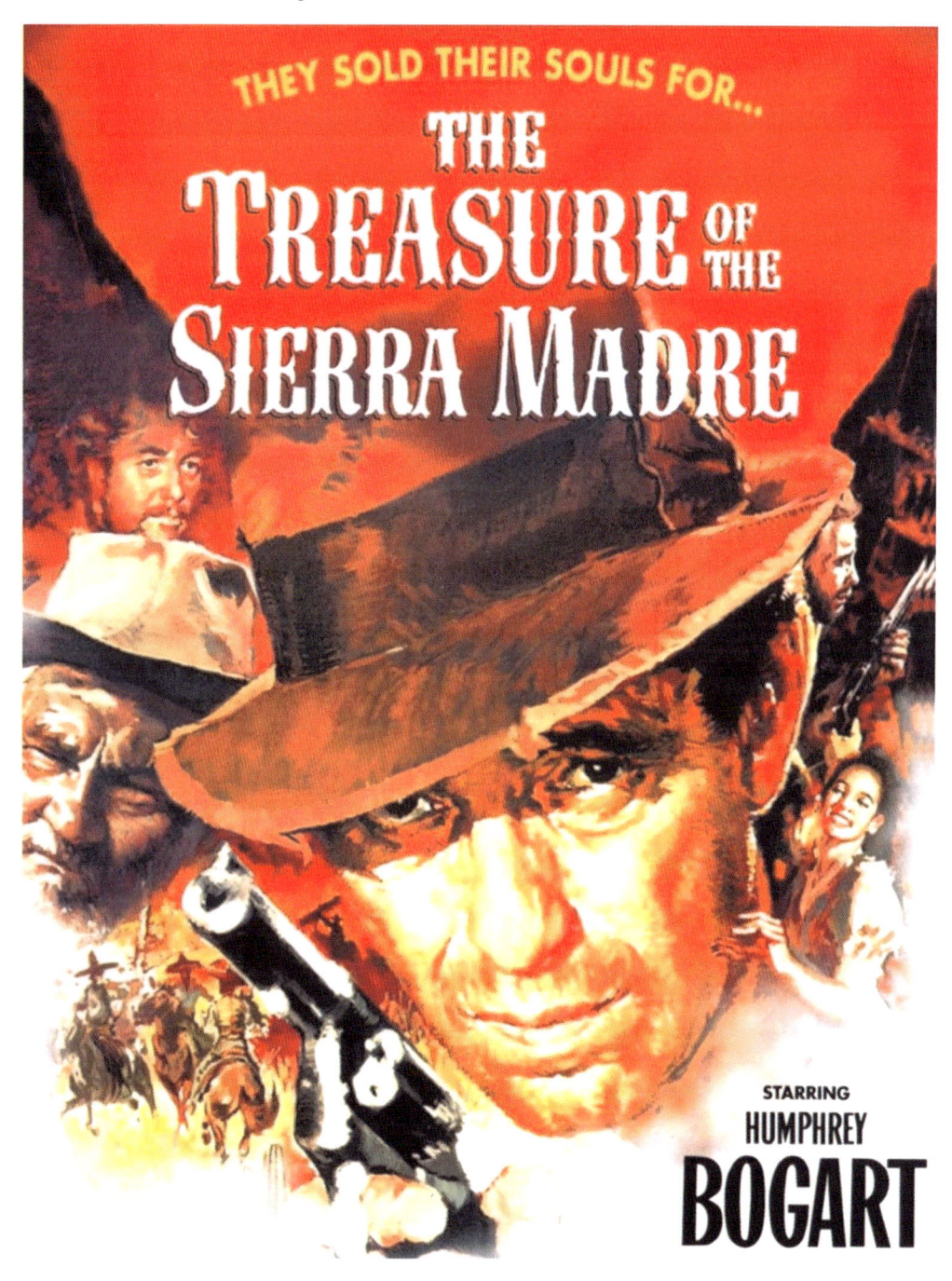

Fred C. Dobbs and Bob Curtin, two Americans searching for work in Mexico, convince an old prospector to help them mine for gold in the Sierra Madre Mountains.

STARRING

Humphrey Bogart
Born: 25th December 1899
Died: 14th January 1957

Character:
Fred C. Dobbs

Screen and stage actor whose performances in films such as The Maltese Falcon (1941), Casablanca (1942) and The Big Sleep (1946) earned him status as a cultural icon. During a 30 year film career he appeared in more than 75 films, receiving three Oscar nominations for Best Actor and winning one for The African Queen (1951). In 1999 the American Film Institute ranked Bogart as the greatest male star of Classic American cinema.

Walter Huston
Born: 5th April 1883
Died: 7th April 1950

Character:
Howard

A Canadian-born American actor and singer. Huston won the Academy Award for Best Supporting Actor for his role in The Treasure Of The Sierra Madre, directed by his son John Huston (who won an Oscar for Best Director thus making them the first father and son to win at the same ceremony). He is a member of the American Theatre Hall of Fame and in 1960 was honoured with a star on the Hollywood Walk of Fame.

Tim Holt
Born: 5th February 1919
Died: 15th February 1973

Character:
Bob Curtin

Film actor best known for his youthful leading roles in dozens of westerns along with his co-starring role in The Treasure Of The Sierra Madre. Holt was a World War II decorated combat veteran flying in the Pacific with the U.S. Army Air Forces as a B-29 bombardier. He was wounded over Tokyo on the last day of the war for which he received a Purple Heart. He was also a recipient of the Distinguished Flying Cross.

TRIVIA

Goofs Although set in Mexico in the 1920s many of the cars on the street in the Tampico scenes are from the 1930s and 1940s.

As Dobbs is looking around trying to find Curtin's body, so that he can bury it, he runs into some bushes. As the camera pans round to follow him you can plainly see where the set ends (a large water tank and a hose are visible to the left).

Interesting Facts A doctor assigned to the film in Mexico had to attend to John Huston one night when he had an adverse reaction to marijuana (having smoked it for the first time with his father). He never touched the stuff again.

CONTINUED

Interesting Facts In his Oscar acceptance speech, Walter Huston said, 'Many many years ago I brought up a boy and I said to him, Son, if you ever become a writer try to write a good part for your old man sometime. Well, by cracky, that's what he did!'

Humphrey Bogart started losing his hair in 1947 partly due to the hormone shots he was taking to improve his chances of having a child with wife Lauren Bacall (although his excessive drinking and lack of vitamin B were probably also factors in his hair loss). He was completely bald by the time he arrived in Mexico for filming. Once on location Bogart started taking vitamin B shots and some of his hair grew back but not enough and he was forced to sport a wig throughout the entire shoot.

John Huston played one of his infamous practical jokes on Bruce Bennett in the campfire scene in which he eats a plate of stew. Bennett knew that his character was supposed to be starving so he wolfed down the food as quickly as possible. Huston then demanded another take and then another. In both extra takes the rapidly filling-up Bennett again had to eat a large plate of stew. Unbeknownst to him Huston had been happy with the first take and the cameras weren't even rolling for the second and the third, he just wanted to see how much food Bennett could eat before he became too stuffed. As soon as the joke was revealed Huston added insult to injury by calling for a lunch break.

Quotes **Bob Curtin:** Wouldn't it be better the way things are to separate tomorrow or even tonight?
Fred C. Dobbs: That would suit you fine wouldn't it?
Bob Curtin: Why me more than you?
Fred C. Dobbs: So you could fall on me from behind, sneak up and shoot me in the back.
Bob Curtin: All right I'll go first.
Fred C. Dobbs: And wait for me on the trail to ambush me?

Bob Curtin: Remember what you said back in Tampico about having to carry that old man on our backs?
Fred C. Dobbs: That was when I took him for an ordinary human being, not part goat.

Easter Parade

Directed by: Charles Walters - Runtime: 107 minutes

A nightclub performer hires a naive chorus girl to become his new dance partner all to make his former partner jealous and to prove he can make any partner a star.

STARRING

Judy Garland
Born: 10th June 1922
Died: 22nd June 1969

Character:
Hannah Brown

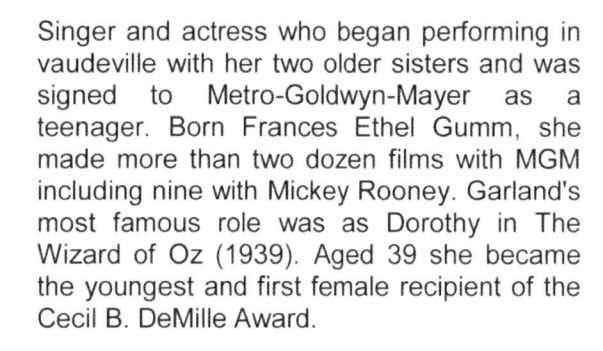

Singer and actress who began performing in vaudeville with her two older sisters and was signed to Metro-Goldwyn-Mayer as a teenager. Born Frances Ethel Gumm, she made more than two dozen films with MGM including nine with Mickey Rooney. Garland's most famous role was as Dorothy in The Wizard of Oz (1939). Aged 39 she became the youngest and first female recipient of the Cecil B. DeMille Award.

Fred Astaire
Born: 10th May 1899
Died: 22nd June 1987

Character:
Don Hewes

Born Frederick Austerlitz, Astaire was an American dancer, choreographer, singer, musician and actor. His stage and subsequent film and television careers spanned a total of 76 years during which he made 31 musical films and several award-winning television specials. He is best known as the dancing partner and on-screen romantic interest of Ginger Rogers.

Peter Lawford
Born: 7th September 1923
Died: 24th December 1984

Character:
Jonathan Harrow III

British actor who lived in the U.S. throughout his adult life. His first major film role was in A Yank At Eton (1942), wherein he played a snobbish bully opposite Mickey Rooney. The film was a smash hit and his performance was widely praised. Lawford was a member of the 'Rat Pack' and brother-in-law to President John F. Kennedy. In later years he was noted more for his off-screen activities as a celebrity than for his acting.

TRIVIA

Goofs

During 'Steppin Out With My Baby', Hewes twirls a girl and her skirt floats up and revealed a black underskirt. However when twirled again she has a bright yellow underskirt.

When a police officer writes Jonathan (Peter Lawford) a ticket for parking beside a fire hydrant and hands over the ticket, he bumps the hydrant causing it to wobble.

While Hannah sings, 'It Only Happens When I Dance With You', she's supposed to be accompanying herself on the piano but her hands never reach the low notes that we hear.

CONTINUED

Interesting Facts

Gene Kelly was originally scheduled to play Don Hewes but he broke his ankle when he stamped his foot in anger after losing a volleyball game. It was at his suggestion that he be replaced by Fred Astaire.

Although she had been a star for years Judy Garland had never met Astaire before and was afraid to speak to him until they were properly introduced.

This film saw the debut of Jules Munshin. He plays the comic waiter who gives very entertaining descriptions of the menu items. A year later he would play one of the three sailors on leave in New York City in the film On The Town (1949) with Gene Kelly and Frank Sinatra.

Ann Miller had to perform her biggest numbers in the film in a back brace. In an interview with Robert Osborne she revealed that she had been thrown down the stairs by her then husband Reese Milner. She was also pregnant at the time and was in a lot of pain.

The song Easter Parade, which inspired the movie, was first sung in Irving Berlin's 1933 Broadway revue As Thousands Cheer, by Marilyn Miller and Clifton Webb. It was inspired by the annual event in New York City where people stroll down Fifth Avenue displaying their new hats (many of them often quite outrageous) and their Easter finery. The song also appeared in the Irving Berlin movie Holiday Inn (1942).

Quotes

Don Hewes: A girl dancer has to be exotic; she has to be a peach.
Hannah Brown: I suppose I'm a lemon!

Hannah Brown: *[her eyes are closed]* What colour are my eyes?
Don Hewes: *[kissing her, causing her to open her eyes in surprise]* Brown.

Don Hewes: Miss Brown, what idiot ever told you you were a dancer?
Hannah Brown: You did.

Sporting Winners

Home Nations Rugby
Ireland

Position	Nation	Played	Won	Draw	Lost	For	Against	Points
1	Ireland	4	4	0	0	36	19	8
2	France	4	2	0	2	40	25	4
3	Scotland	4	2	0	2	15	31	4
4	Wales	4	1	1	2	23	20	3
5	England	4	0	1	3	16	35	1

The 1948 Five Nations Championship was the nineteenth series of the rugby union Five Nations Championship. Including the previous incarnations as the Home Nations and Five Nations, this was the fifty-fourth series of the northern hemisphere rugby union championship. Ten matches were played between the 1st January and 29th March. It was contested by England, France, Ireland, Scotland and Wales.

Date	Team	Score	Team	Location
01/01/1948	France	6-13	Ireland	Paris
17/01/1948	England	3-3	Wales	London
24/01/1948	Scotland	9-8	France	Edinburgh
07/02/1948	Wales	14-0	Scotland	Cardiff
14/02/1948	England	10-11	Ireland	London
14/02/1948	Wales	3-11	France	Cardiff
28/02/1948	Ireland	6-0	Scotland	Dublin
13/03/1948	Ireland	6-3	Wales	Belfast
20/03/1948	Scotland	6-3	England	Edinburgh
29/03/1948	France	15-0	England	Paris

Calcutta Cup Winners

Scotland

The Calcutta Cup was first awarded in 1879 and is the rugby union trophy awarded to the winner of the match (currently played as part of the Six Nations Championship) between England and Scotland.

1948 British Grand Prix
Luigi Villoresi

Maserati 4CLT/48 driver Luigi Villoresi wins the British Grand Prix in a time of 3h 18m 3s.

The 1948 British Grand Prix motor race was held at Silverstone Airfield, Northamptonshire on the 2nd October. The race was held over 65 laps of the 3.67 mile circuit giving a total race distance of 238.55 miles. After starting from the back of the grid in 24th position (due to missing the official practice) the race was won by Maserati driver Luigi Villoresi for Italy. Second place was taken by another Maserati driver Alberto Ascari (Italy) and third place by English Racing Automobiles (ERA) driver Bob Gerard (UK). The race meeting marked the opening of the Silverstone Circuit.

Snooker
Fred Davis

✚ Fred Davis - 84
✖ Walter Donaldson - 61

The 1948 World Snooker Championship was a tournament held at the Leicester Square Hall in London from the 19th April to 1st May. Davis won his first World title by defeating Donaldson 81-64 in the final and also made the highest break of the tournament with 109.

GRAND NATIONAL
SHEILA'S COTTAGE

The 1948 Grand National was the 104th renewal of this world famous horse race and took place at Aintree Racecourse near Liverpool on the 20th March. 50/1 winner Shelia's Cottage was trained by Neville Crump (for owner John Proctor) and ridden by Arthur Thompson. Sheila's Cottage became the first mare to win the National for 46 years and only the 12th in the long history of the steeplechase.

	Name	Jockey	Age	Weight	Odds
1st	Shelia's Cottage	Arthur Thompson	9	10st 7lbs	50/1
2nd	First Of The Dandies	Jimmy Brogan	11	10st 4lbs	25/1
3rd	Cromwell	Anthony Mildmay	7	10st 11lb	33/1

43 Runners - 14 Finished / 3 Pulled Up / 21 Fell / 1 Brought Down / 1 Refused
1 Unseated Rider / 1 Ran Out / 1 Carried Out

EPSOM DERBY
MY LOVE

The Derby Stakes is Britain's richest horse race and the most prestigious of the country's five Classics. First run in 1780 this Group 1 flat horse race is open to three year old thoroughbred colts and fillies. It is run at Epsom Downs in Surrey over a distance of one mile, four furlongs and 10 yards (2,423 metres) and is scheduled for early June each year.

Photo: French-bred, thoroughbred racehorse and sire My Love (1945-1962), ridden by Rae Johnstone, seen here winning the 1948 Epson Derby from second placed Royal Drake.

Football League Champions

England

Pos.	Team	F	A	Points
1	**Arsenal**	**81**	**32**	**59**
2	Manchester United	81	48	52
3	Burnley	56	43	52
4	Derby County	77	57	50
5	Wolverhampton Wanderers	83	70	47

Scotland

Pos.	Team	F	A	Points
1	**Hibernian**	**86**	**27**	**48**
2	Rangers	64	28	46
3	Partick Thistle	61	42	36
4	Dundee	67	51	33
5	St Mirren	54	58	31

FA Cup Winners - Manchester United

Manchester United 4-2 Blackpool

Jack Rowley 28', 70'
Stan Pearson 80'
John Anderson 82'

Eddie Shimwell 12' (pen)
Stan Mortensen 35'

Referee: C. J. Barrick - Attendance: 99,842

The 1948 FA Cup Final took place on the 24th April at Wembley Stadium. United, who had not appeared in an FA Cup Final for 39 years, won the game 4-2. Blackpool's Eddie Shimwell became the first ever full-back to score a goal in a Wembley Cup Final.

The British Open - Golf

Henry Cotton

The 1948 Open Championship was the 77th Open Championship and was held between the 30th June and 2nd July at Muirfield in Gullane, East Lothian, Scotland. 41 year old Henry Cotton won his third and final Open title, five strokes ahead of runner-up and defending champion Fred Daly, to take the Claret Jug and winner's prize money of £150.

Cricket

The Ashes

England 0 - 4 Australia

Position	Teams	Ground	Result	Winning Margin
1st Test	England v Australia	Trent Bridge	Australia	8 wickets
2nd Test	England v Australia	Lord's	Australia	409 runs
3rd Test	England v Australia	Old Trafford	Draw	
4th Test	England v Australia	Headingley	Australia	7 wickets
5th Test	England v Australia	The Oval	Australia	Innings & 149 runs

The 1948 Ashes series was that year's edition of the long-standing cricket rivalry between England and Australia. Starting on the 10th June 1948 England and Australia played five Tests. Australia had not lost a Test since the Second World War and were justified strong favourites when winning series 4-0 and retaining The Ashes.

Photo: Australia's captain Don Bradman gets bowled out second ball for a duck with a googly in the 5th Test at The Oval. This was his last at international match and with 6996 Test career runs he had only needed four runs to average 100 in Test cricket.

WIMBLEDON

Photo 1: Bob Falkenburg playing against John Bromwich at Wimbledon (1949).
Photo 2: Louise Brough (left) and Doris Hart holding bouquets before their Singles Final.

Mens Singles Champion - Bob Falkenburg - United States
Ladies Singles Champion - Louise Brough - United States

The 1948 Wimbledon Championships took place on the outdoor grass courts at the All England Lawn Tennis and Croquet Club in Wimbledon, London. The tournament ran from the 21st June until the 2nd July. It was the 62nd staging of the Wimbledon Championships and the third Grand Slam tennis event of 1948.

Men's Singles Final:

Country	Player	Set 1	Set 2	Set 3	Set 4	Set 5
United States	Bob Falkenburg	7	0	6	3	7
Australia	John Bromwich	5	6	2	6	5

Women's Singles Final:

Country	Player	Set 1	Set 2
United States	Louise Brough	6	8
United States	Doris Hart	3	6

Men's Doubles Final:

Country	Players	Set 1	Set 2	Set 3	Set 4
Australia	John Bromwich / Frank Sedgman	5	7	7	9
United States	Tom Brown / Gardnar Mulloy	7	5	5	7

Women's Doubles Final:

Country	Players	Set 1	Set 2	Set 3
United States	Louise Brough / Margaret Osborne duPont	6	3	6
United States	Doris Hart / Patricia Todd	3	6	3

Mixed Doubles Final:

Country	Players	Set 1	Set 2	Set 3
United States / Australia	Louise Brough / John Bromwich	6	3	6
United States / Australia	Doris Hart / Frank Sedgman	2	6	3

1948 Summer Olympics

The 1948 Summer Olympics, officially known as the Games of the XIV Olympiad, were held in London from the 29th July to the 14th August. The Games had 4,104 athletes from 59 National Olympic Committees participating in a total of 136 events. These were the first Summer Olympics since 1936 due to WWII and had the highest number of nations represented at any Games to date (Germany and Japan were refused permission to participate and although the USSR was invited it chose not to send any athletes).

Medals table;

Rank	Nation	Gold	Silver	Bronze	Total
1	**United States**	**38**	**27**	**19**	**84**
2	Sweden	16	11	17	44
3	France	10	6	13	29
4	Hungary	10	5	12	27
5	Italy	8	11	8	27
12	Great Britain & NI	3	14	6	23

One of the star performers at the Games was Dutch sprinter Fanny Blankers-Koen. Dubbed The Flying Housewife, the 30-year-old mother of two won four gold medals in athletics. In the decathlon, American Bob Mathias became the youngest male ever to win an Olympic gold medal at the age of 17.

British Medals;

Sport	1	2	3
Rowing	2	1	0
Sailing	1	0	0
Athletics	0	6	1
Cycling	0	3	2
Boxing	0	2	0

Sport	1	2	3
Weightlifting	0	1	1
Field Hockey	0	1	0
Equestrian	0	0	1
Swimming	0	0	1
Medal Totals	3	14	6

The Cost Of Living
Comparison Chart

	1948 Price	1948 Price Today (Including inflation)	2017 Price	Real Term % Change
3 Bedroom House	£2100	£75,426	£226,000	+199.6%
Weekly Income	£4 10s 1d	£161.78	£530	+276.1%
Pint Of Beer	10d	£1.50	£3.47	+131.3%
Cheese (lb)	1s 11d	£3.44	£3.25	-5.5%
Bacon (lb)	2s 1d	£3.74	£3.63	-2.9%
The Beano	2d	30p	£2.50	+733.3%

only 1 point

ROWNTREE'S FRUIT GUMS

soothe and refresh

Tubes 2½d. (and only ONE Personal Point)

When the good news gets around

LOOK TO Libby's FOR PERFECTION

Just now your quest for the famous "Blue and White" Label may not be successful. But one day the good news will get around that Libby's Bartlett Pears, with all their delicate flavour intact, are again freely available and your good taste will be rewarded.

LOOK FOR THE FAMOUS 'BLUE AND WHITE' LABEL
LIBBY, McNEILL & LIBBY LTD., LONDON, E.C.3.

---

felt TO BE BETTER..

You simply won't feel a Brylshave. What you will feel is the skin soft, supple and refreshed *after* the shave — and it's remarkably quick too. Yes, Brylshave is the perfect shave. Try it and prove it. In jars and tubes 1/11d.

BRUSHLESS Brylshave

"SURPRISINGLY COMFORTABLE"
Made by the makers of 'Brylcreem'

They've all been picked for **Batchelor's** where the best *foods* go!

ENGLISH CANNED FRUITS · VEGETABLES · SOUPS

GIVE INSECTS THE NEW ONE-TWO!
★ PROTECT FOOD & CLOTHES WITH

Double-action FLIT

1. INSTANT KILLING ACTION WITH PYRETHRUM
2. LASTING ACTION WITH D.D.T.

(1) Spray Flit in the air after closing windows and doors. Spray Flit in wardrobes, for moths.

(2) Spray Flit 3 or 4 times on walls and ceilings. The DDT kills insects touching sprayed surfaces.

FLIT LIQUID AND POWDER

CHIVERS JAMS ARE MADE IN SILVER LINED PANS

The favourite for tea-time **CHIVERS JAMS** are on sale everywhere

★

For a change, we recommend Chivers Plum Jam. Plenty of fruit—Lovely flavour.

CHIVERS & SONS LTD., The Orchard Factory, Histon, Cambridge

SHOPPING

Fry's Cocoa (per lb)	2s 8d
Suttons Fruit Squash (bottle)	3s
Grape-Nuts (12 helpings)	10d
Rowntree's Kitkat Chocolate Crisp	2d
Victory V Gums & Lozenges (4½oz)	1s 1½d
Rowntrees Fruit Gums (tube)	2½d
Mars Crest Whipped Nut Bar	4½d
Scott & Turner's Rose Hip Syrup (bottle)	1s 9d
Dip Permanent Plastic Starch (bottle)	2s 3d
Brylshave Brushless Shave	1s 11d
Gillette Razor Blades (x10)	2s 11d
Fairy Soap (per tablet)	5¾d
Brylcreem (jar)	1s 11½d
Amami Wave Set	2s 6½d
Silktona Leg Make-Up (large sachet)	8d
Johnson & Johnson Tek Toothbrush (bristle)	2s 6d
Gibbs SR Toothpaste (large size)	2s 3d
Colgate Toothpaste	1s 3½d
Phillip's Dental Magnesia (tube)	1s 6d
Phensic Cold Relief (large)	3s 8d
Beecham's Powders (carton of 6)	1s 6d
Lixen - The Good Natured Laxative (bottle)	3d
Peps (per box)	1s 7d
Kiwi Boot Polish (tin)	8d

DAILY MIRROR ECONOMIC ANALYSIS

FOOD: Here's Our Target

LAST year's weather—frost, flood and drought—means less food this year. But we propose to increase production like this:

	1947 Tons	1948 Target Tons
Bread Grains	1,694,000	2,484,000
Other Grains	4,469,000	5,190,000
Potatoes	7,766,000	9,961,000
Sugar Beet	2,886,000	3,600,000

Belts Will Be Tighter

The figures below (decimal points have been avoided) show, in round terms, how much food we used to get and how much we can expect this year. The figures are in lbs. per head of the population.

	Pre-war	1947	1948		Pre-war	1947	1948
Dairy products	38	49	46	Sugar and syrups	110	85	76
Meat	110	82	67	Tomatoes and fresh fruit	142	127	108
Fish, game and poultry	33	36	34	Vegetables	107	118	82
Oils and fats	45	34	35	Grain products	218	241	248

IN CALORIES IT MEANS THAT WE SHALL FALL FROM AN AVERAGE OF 3,000 CALORIES A DAY BEFORE THE WAR AND 2,880 LAST YEAR, TO 2,681 IN 1948.

THE JOBS THAT NEED YOU

IN the table below you can see how the workers are distributed in the main industries. The last column shows the target for the end of this year. All these jobs need MORE workers:

	1939	End 1947	Target End 1948
Coal	735,000	718,000	750,000
Transport and Shipping	1,233,000	1,438,000	1,460,000
Agriculture	910,000	1,055,000	1,110,000
Metals and Engineering	2,267,000	2,876,000	2,900,000
Textiles	798,000	652,000	760,000

THE JOBS YOU MUST LEAVE

AND these trades must have FEWER workers:

	1939	End 1947	Target End 1948
Building and Civil Engineering	1,310,000	1,364,000	1,200,000
Clothing	1,005,000	831,000	800,000
Food, Drink and Tobacco	654,000	623,000	600,000
Distribution	2,887,000	2,351,000	2,320,000

The number of men in the building industry, says the White Paper, is larger than the present supplies of materials can sustain.

WHAT WE MUST PRODUCE

COAL, steel, textiles. Britain's whole future depends on those three things. Here is the production target:

	Actual production 1947	Target 1948
COAL:	Tons	Tons
Deep Mined	186,300,000	200,000,000
Opencast	10,200,000	11,000,000
STEEL	12,724,000	14,000,000
TEXTILES:	lb.	lb.
Cotton Yarn	828,000,000	1,000,000,000
Worsted Yarn	170,000,000	204,000,000
Woollen and Worsted Cloth	260,000,000	300,000,000
Rayon	85,000,000	120,000,000

VOLUNTEERS NOT ENOUGH?

TO get that extra COAL means recruiting 102,000 new workers for the mines because about 70,000 men now working will retire during the year owing to age, ill-health or accident.

To get the STEEL we need every ounce of scrap metal, more coke and all-out production all the year.

To get the TEXTILES means increasing the number of workers like this:

	Number working in Dec. 1947	Target for End of 1948
Cotton	267,000	325,000
Woollen and Worsted	178,000	200,000
Other Textiles	207,000	235,000

A BIG JOB! AND THE WHITE PAPER SAYS FRANKLY THAT IT IS UNLIKELY THAT THE TARGET FIGURE CAN BE REACHED BY VOLUNTARY RECRUITMENT AND BRINGING IN FOREIGN WORKERS.

"Further measures," it says, "may be required to restrain the growth of other industries and services in the textile areas and encourage the transfer of unused textile plant to other areas."

SETTING NEW STANDARDS

OF COMFORT AND BEAUTY

FOR MANY YEARS TO COME

THE NEW

MINX MAGNIFICENT

A full-sized family car, outstandingly new in design and construction, lighter in weight

Independent front suspension	Exceptional covered luggage accommodation
Opticurve windscreen	New and improved steering
Unique driving control and vision	Everything, bonnet, interior, luggage and spare wheel, under lock and key
Bench type front seat	
New styled coachwork of brilliant design	Powered by the famous, fully-proved Hillman Minx engine
No-draught ventilation	
Proved Synchromatic Gear Control	Radio and controlled air conditioning available as optional extras

HILLMAN MINX

Saloon · Convertible Coupé · Estate Car

A PRODUCT OF THE ROOTES GROUP

See them at INTERNATIONAL MOTOR EXHIBITION, EARL'S COURT, OCT. 27—NOV. 6, 1948. Stand No. 160

56

OTHER PRICES

Aston Martin 2 Litre Sports Car	£2332
Jaguar 3.5 Litre Saloon	£1263
MG Midget TC	£528
Sugden's Furs Beaver Lamb Swagger Coat	£32 17s
Corot Bond Street Ladies 'Diane' Suit	£5 16s
Jacoll Hat	11s 9d
John White Mens Shoes	£2 8s 6d
Paris Professional Road Racing Bicycle	£11 18s 6d
Qualcast Clothes Wringer	£4 15s
Hardy & Co Interior Sprung Mattress	15gns
Hardwearing Tablecloth (42in x 42in)	15s 6d
Baird Townsman 12in B&W Television	72gns
Goblin Electric Vacuum Cleaner	£12 12s
Columbia Record Player	£8 10s
Walnut Veneer KB Radio	£21 10s
Ultra Radio	£15 15s
H. Samuel Lucky Wedding Rings (from…)	£1 11s
Mentmore '46' Gold Filled Cap Pen	£3
Dinky Toy Armstrong-Siddeley Coupe	2s 6d
Dinky Toy Single Deck Bus	2s 10d
Dewar's White Label Scotch Whisky (bottle)	£1 11s
Booth's Dry Gin (half bottle)	15s 9d
VP Wine (bottle)	9s
Idris Non Alcoholic Ginger Wine (bottle)	2s 6d
Minors Cigarettes (20)	2s 7d

THE MONEY

Money Conversion Table

Old Money		Equivalent Today
Farthing	¼d	0.1p
Half Penny	½d	0.21p
Penny	1d	0.42p
Threepence	3d	1.25p
Sixpence	6d	2.5p
Shilling	1s	5p
Florin	2s	10p
Half Crown	2s 6d	12.5p
Crown	5s	25p
Ten Shillings	10s	50p
Pound	20s	£1
Guinea	21s	£1.05

Gosh Mummy, can I eat it all?

IT'S love at first sight between any youngster and a Rowntree's Jelly. And at the very first bite children are quick to taste the *real fruit* flavour. Rowntree's Jellies are so easy to make that you needn't wait for a party to make their eyes big with expectation! Ask your grocer for Rowntree's Table Jellies.

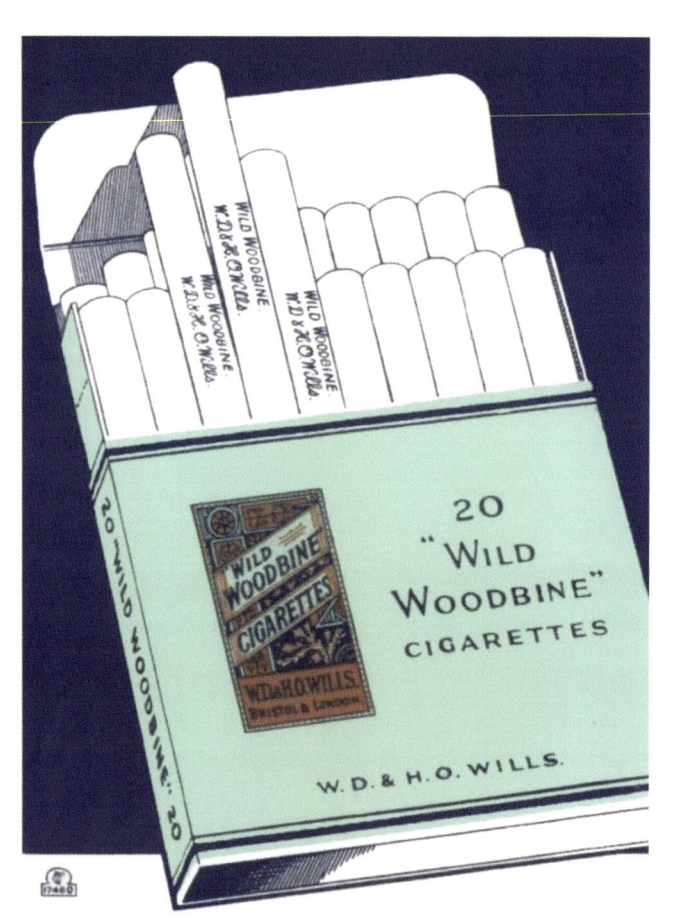

20 "WILD WOODBINE" CIGARETTES

W.D. & H.O. WILLS

WOODBINE
– the great little cigarette

HOW TO HAVE lovelier legs THIS SUMMER

You can have silken-smooth, bronze-tanned legs from the start of your holidays. Simply use Silktona, the latest, most glamorous Leg Make-Up. Silktona gives your legs a beautiful, matt finish, that shows off snappy beachwear and play suits perfectly. Easily applied. Get Silktona *today!*

Large Sachet 8d.
(Enough for 24 applications of glamour!)
From Woolworths, Timothy Whites and all chemists.

Silktona
LEG MAKE-UP

Can I smoke less tobacco?

And still enjoy 20 a day?

20 good cigarettes?

Yes! mine's a MINOR

20 for 2/7

PLAIN OR CORK TIPPED

ISSUED BY GODFREY PHILLIPS LIMITED

For smoother hands on washday — try this

Change to Fairy household Soap—and you'll get through the weekly wash more easily, and find your hands smoother, because it...

- Combines high cleaning power with maximum blandness.
- Contains no Soda.
- Is absolutely mild—cannot harm delicate skin.

MILD AS ANY TOILET SOAP

Change to FAIRY soap

CONTAINS NO SODA . 5½d. PER TABLET

Kiss the Girl WITH THE MAGNESIA SMILE

Phillips' Dental Magnesia

All eyes on the girl with the *magnesia smile!* Such sparkling white teeth. Such healthy pink gums. Such sweet breath. Only Phillips' Dental Magnesia can give you that magnesia smile because only this toothpaste contains * 'Milk of Magnesia' which many dentists advise for neutralizing harmful mouth acids.

1/6 per tube
Extra large 2/6

* 'Milk of Magnesia' is the trade mark of Phillips' preparation of magnesia.

1948

METTOY PLAYTHINGS

MADE BY CRAFTSMEN IN GREAT BRITAIN

MODERN MECHANICAL TOYS

It's never too warm (or cold) TO ENJOY **Victory·V** GUMS & LOZENGES
4 ozs. 1'1½d.   NO POINTS

Maintaining the Breed

Safety fast!

Your MG deserves regular grooming too. It will run for thousands of miles with little attention, but a regular check-up will ensure matchless MG performance. Your MG dealer is ready to do this, with "MG-trained" advice and service.

THE MG CAR COMPANY LTD., ABINGDON-ON-THAMES — A NUFFIELD PRODUCT

Overseas Business : Nuffield Exports Ltd., Oxford, and 41 Piccadilly, London, W.1

Printed in Great Britain
by Amazon